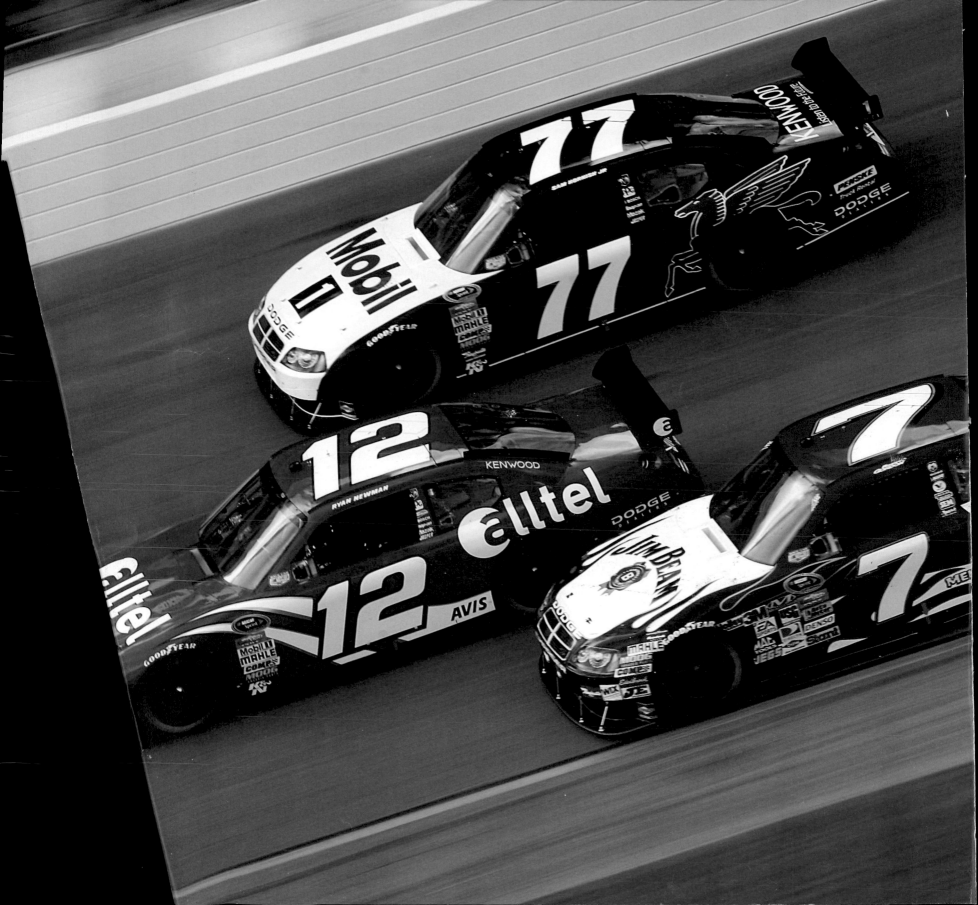

TOP SPEEDS

HORSE — 75 KM (46 MILES) PER HOUR

ELECTRIC SKATEBOARD — 37 KM (23 MILES) PER HOUR

DOG — 70 KM (43.5 MILES) PER HOUR

STOCK CAR — 358 KM (222.6 MILES) PER HOUR

RABBIT — 72 KM (45 MILES) PER HOUR

HUMAN — 45 KM (28 MILES) PER HOUR

BICYCLE — 132 KM (82

NOW THAT'S FAST!

STOCK CARS

KATE RIGGS

FRANKLIN WATTS
LONDON • SYDNEY

First published in the UK in 2011 by
Franklin Watts
338 Euston Road
London NW1 3BH

Franklin Watts Australia
Level 17/207 Kent Street
Sydney NSW 2000

First published by Creative Education,
an imprint of the Creative Company.
Copyright © 2010 Creative Education
International copyright reserved in all countries.
No part of this book may be reproduced in any
form without written permission from
the publisher.

ISBN 978 1 4451 0588 8
Dewey number: 629.2'28

A CIP catalogue record for this book
is available from the British Library.

Printed in China

Franklin Watts is a division of
Hachette Children's Books,
an Hachette UK company.
www.hachette.co.uk

Book and cover design by Blue Design
(www.bluedes.com)
Art direction by Rita Marshall

Photographs by Dreamstime (Actionsports,
walleyelj), Getty Images (John Harrelson/NASCAR,
Robert Laberge/Nascar, Nick Laham, RacingOne,
Jamie Squire, Matthew Stockman, Todd Warshaw/
NASCAR, Frank Whitney), istockphoto (Michael
Krinke).

Every atttempt has been made to clear copyright.
Should there be any inadvertent omission, please
contact the publisher for rectification.

A stock car is a kind of racing car. Stock cars have **engines** that are **designed** to make them go fast. Most stock cars can zoom along at over 300 kilometres per hour (kph)!

A stock car engine. Stock cars have more powerful engines than normal cars.

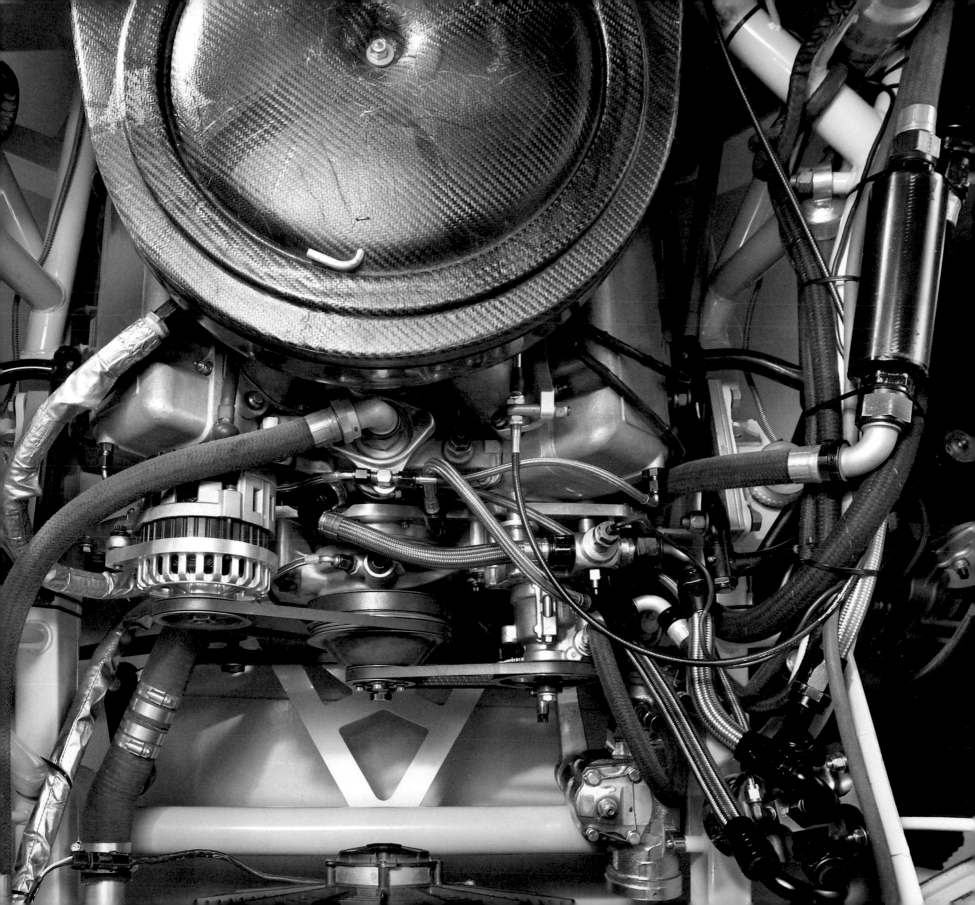

Stock cars look like normal cars,
but they are designed for racing:
they are lighter, so they can go
faster. Each car has a **roll cage**.
This is a frame that helps keep
the driver safe if the car crashes.
The roof of a stock car also has a
safety device to stop the car from
flipping over.

There is not much space for the
driver inside a stock car!

A stock car race at the famous
Daytona International Speedway
in Florida, USA.

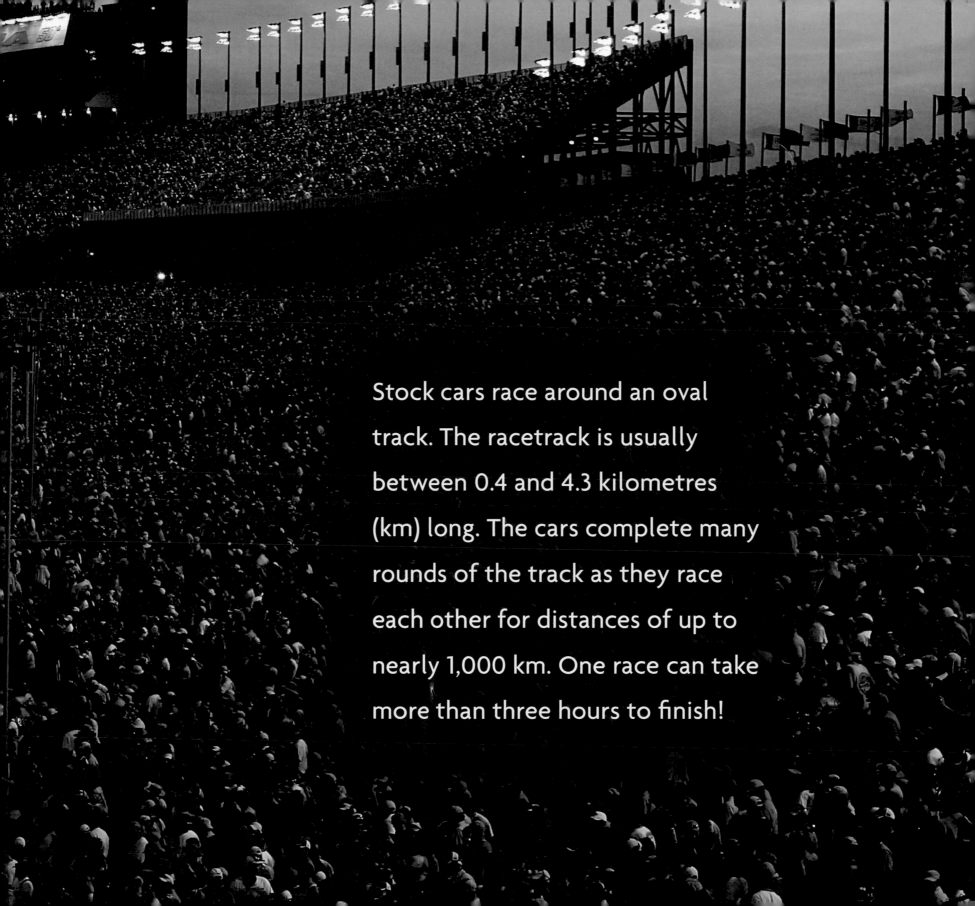

Stock cars race around an oval track. The racetrack is usually between 0.4 and 4.3 kilometres (km) long. The cars complete many rounds of the track as they race each other for distances of up to nearly 1,000 km. One race can take more than three hours to finish!

Superspeedways are longer race-tracks (over 3 km). Stock cars that race on these tracks have a part added to their engines. A piece of metal called a restrictor plate stops the cars from going at more than 310 kph. This makes the races safer.

Teams of workers called crews work on the cars during superspeedway races to keep them running safely.

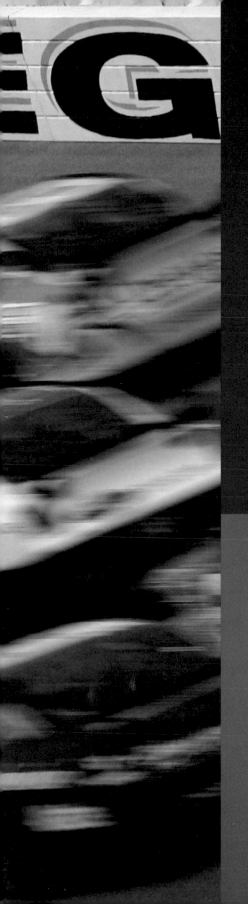

When stock cars race on superspeedways, they zoom around the curves. Sometimes they bunch together. Unlike other types of racing, some contact between the cars is allowed, so drivers can jostle other cars out of the way.

Stock cars squeeze together in a tight race at Talladega Superspeedway in Alabama, USA.

15

The National Association for Stock Car Auto Racing (NASCAR) was formed in the USA in 1948. It organises stock car races across the USA and Canada. Today, it holds over 1,500 races a year. The most famous **series** of NASCAR races is called the Sprint Cup.

A stock car race at Daytona Beach, Florida, in the 1940s.

According to NASCAR rules, all stock cars are made the same way and have the same basic design. That way, all the cars have the same chance of winning, and races are close and exciting.

Today, NASCAR is big business.
Its races are broadcast in over 150
countries around the world to an
audience of millions. Companies
known as **sponsors** can pay to
show their name on the side of
a car and on the driver's and
crew's kit.

This NASCAR team is sponsored by
Pennzoil, a motor oil company.

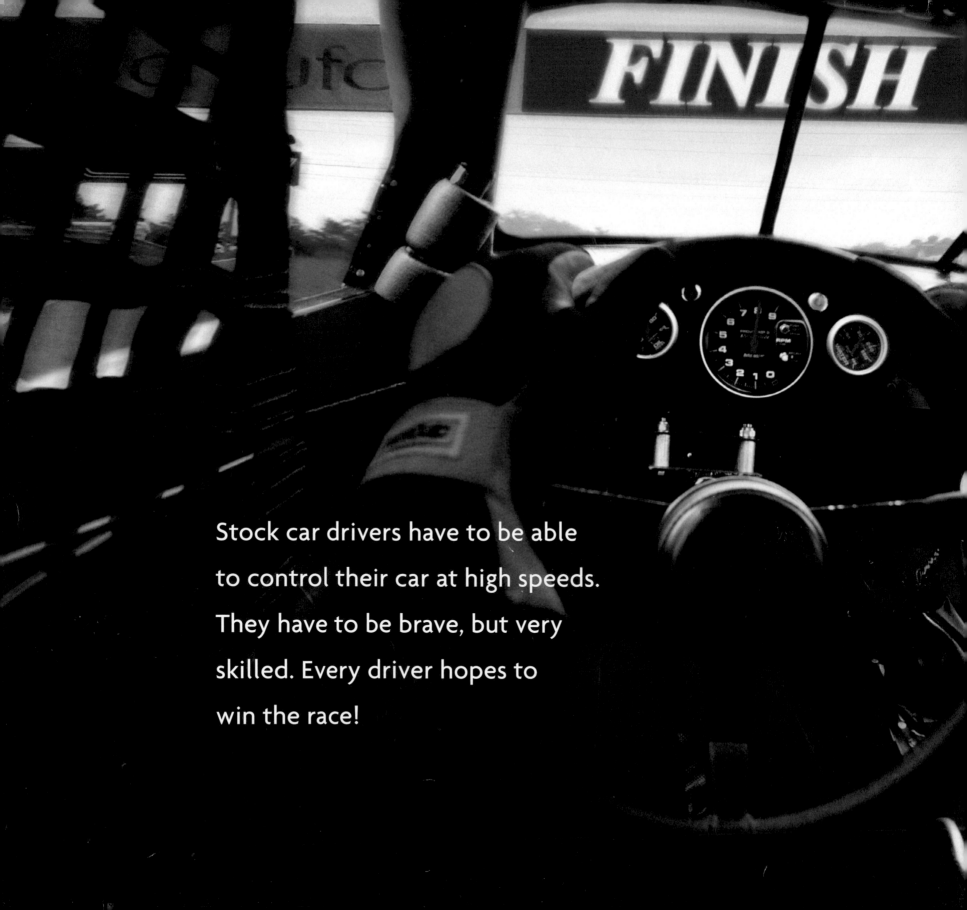

Stock car drivers have to be able to control their car at high speeds. They have to be brave, but very skilled. Every driver hopes to win the race!

Fast Facts

Jimmie Johnson is one of the most famous stock car drivers in the world. Johnson has so far won five NASCAR Sprint Cup Championships in a row (2006–2010), becoming the first driver to do so.

Stock cars can go as fast as 335 km per hour in some NASCAR races.

Stock car racing is popular around the world in countries as varied as the UK, New Zealand and Brazil, as well as the USA.

NASCAR runs a huge range of competitions, including a series of races for pick-up trucks!

Glossary

design – a plan that shows how something will look and how it will work

engines – machines that make vehicles move

roll cage – a frame of metal bars that is built into the sides and top of a stock car

series – a set of events

sponsors –companies that support a racing team with money in return for advertising their name or logo

superspeedways – the longest racetracks. They are usually between three and four kilometres long.

Read More about It

Motorsports: Stock Cars by Clive Gifford (Franklin Watts, 2009)

Great Sporting Events: Motorsports by Clive Gifford (Franklin Watts, 2010)

Website

KidzWorld NASCAR trivia

http://www.kidzworld.com/quiz/4479-quiz-nascar-trivia

This site has a fun quiz about NASCAR.

Index